AF606899

GARBAGE TRUCKS

WORKING TRUCKS

PAUL ZACHARY

EZ READERS

Creating Young Nonfiction Readers

EZ Readers lets children delve into nonfiction at beginning reading levels. Young readers are introduced to new concepts, facts, ideas, and vocabulary.

Tips for Reading Nonfiction with Beginning Readers

Talk about Nonfiction
Begin by explaining that nonfiction books give us information that is true. The book will be organized around a specific topic or idea, and we may learn new facts through reading.

Look at the Parts
Most nonfiction books have helpful features. Our *EZ Readers* include a Contents page, an index, a picture glossary, and color photographs. Share the purpose of these features with your reader.

Contents
Located at the front of a book, the Contents displays a list of the big ideas within the book and where to find them.

Index
An index is an alphabetical list of topics and the page numbers where they are found.

Picture Glossary
Located at the back of the book, a picture glossary contains key words/phrases that are related to the topic.

Photos/Charts
A lot of information can be found by "reading" the charts and photos found within nonfiction text. Help your reader learn more about the different ways information can be displayed.

With a little help and guidance about reading nonfiction, you can feel good about introducing a young reader to the world of *EZ Readers* nonfiction books.

Mitchell Lane
PUBLISHERS

2001 SW 31st Avenue
Hallandale, FL 33009
www.mitchelllane.com

First Edition, 2019.

Author: Paul Zachary
Designer: Ed Morgan
Editor: Sharon F. Doorasamy

Names/credits:
Title: Garbage Trucks / by Paul Zachary
Description: Hallandale, FL :
Mitchell Lane Publishers, [2019]

Series: Working Trucks

Library bound ISBN: 9781680202984

eBook ISBN: 9781680202991

EZ readers is an imprint of
Mitchell Lane Publishers

Photo credits: Getty Images, Freepik.com, flaticon.com

Library of Congress Cataloging-in-Publication Data
Names: Zachary, Paul, author.
Title: Garbage trucks / by Paul Zachary.
Description: First edition. | Hallandale, FL : Mitchell Lane Publishers, [2019] | Series: Working trucks | Includes index.
Identifiers: LCCN 2018016798| ISBN 9781680202984 (library bound) | ISBN 9781680202991 (ebook)
Subjects: LCSH: Refuse collection vehicles—Juvenile literature.
Classification: LCC TD792 .Z33 2019 | DDC 628.4/420284—dc23
LC record available at https://lccn.loc.gov/2018016798

CONTENTS

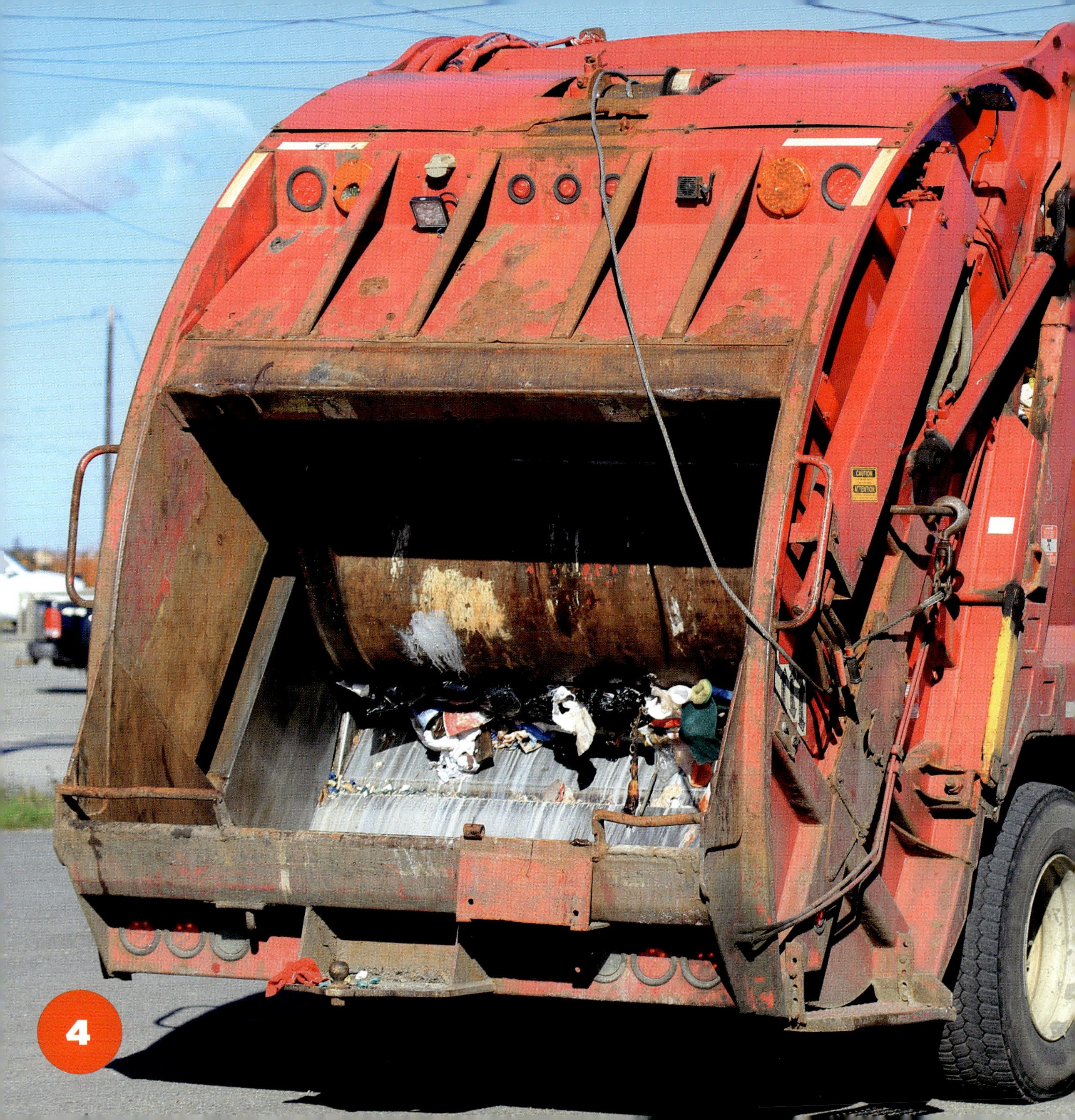
CAUTION
ATTENTION

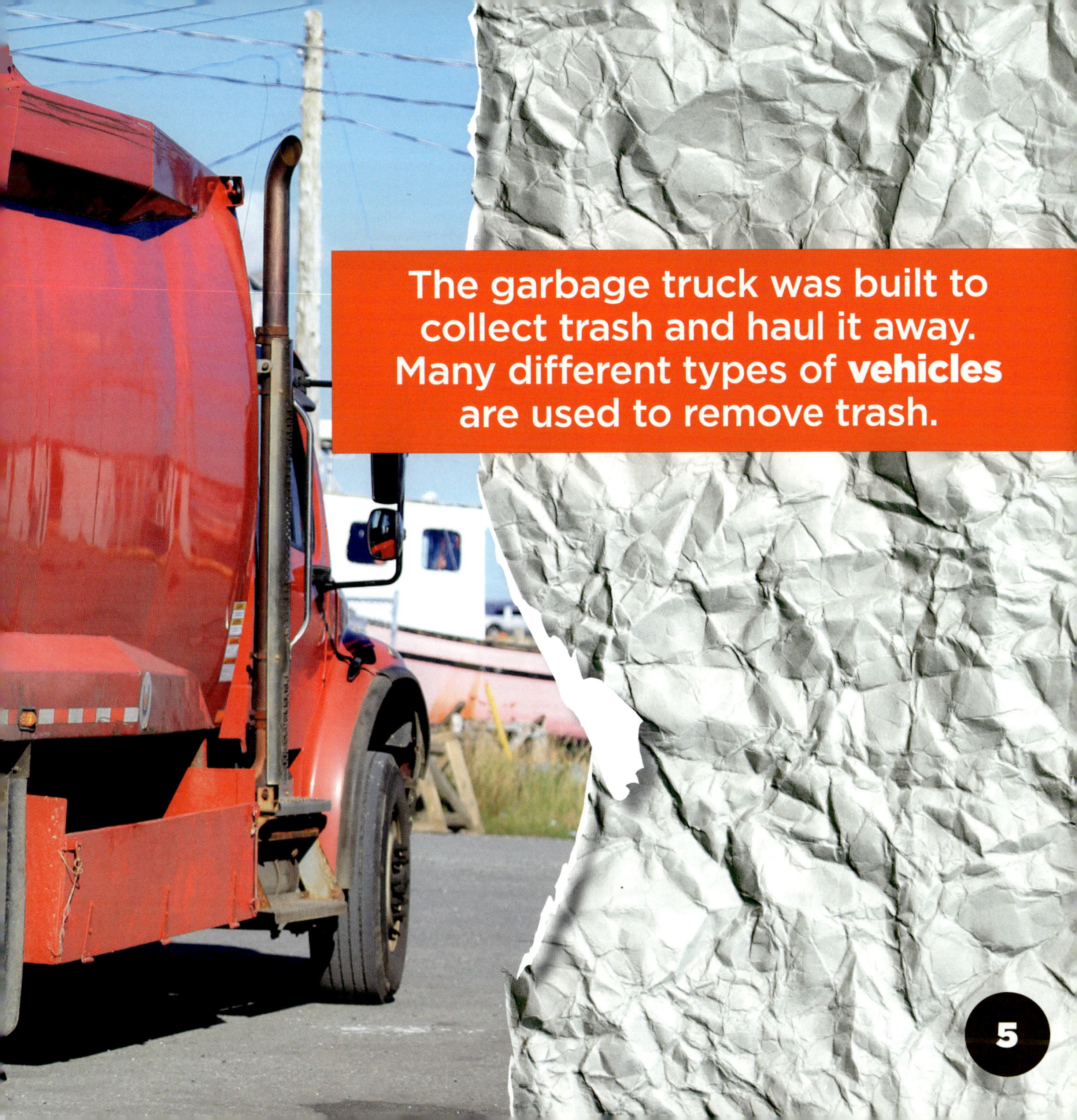

The garbage truck was built to collect trash and haul it away. Many different types of **vehicles** are used to remove trash.

DANGER

Front loaders generally service **commercial** businesses using large waste containers with lids known as dumpsters.

STAY BACK

Rear loaders have an opening at the back of the truck that accepts trash bags or the contents of bins into it.

A sand cleaning machine drags a **sifting device** across the beach sand to remove trash.

A garbage **scow** is used to **transport** garbage across waterways. It is often towed by tugboats.

A landfill site is used for the disposal of waste materials and is the oldest form of waste **treatment**.

Garbage trucks take their trash to **landfill** sites and **dispose** of the waste materials.

The United States creates so much trash that many states have passed laws about recycling.

Plastic
Glass
Metal

Recycling is a process to change waste into new products that helps prevent so much waste.

GLOSSARY

commercial
The activity of providing goods and services for money

dispose
The act of getting rid of something

landfill
An area that has been filled in with trash

scow
A large flat bottom boat

sifting device
A device used to separate sand from trash

transport
To carry something from one place to another

vehicles
A car or truck used to move people or things

waste treatment
The collection, removal, processing, and disposal of trash

INTERESTING FACTS

Most communities spend more money to deal with trash than they spend for school books and libraries.

The energy used to create and distribute junk mail in the United States for one day could heat 250,000 homes.

INDEX